THE ESSENTIAL COLLE

JOPLIN

GOLD

Published by:
Chester Music Limited,
8/9 Frith Street, London W1D 3JB, England.

Exclusive Distributors:
Music Sales Limited,
Distribution Centre, Newmarket Road, Bury St Edmunds, Suffolk IP33 3YB, England.
Music Sales Corporation,
257 Park Avenue South, New York, NY10010, United States of America.
Music Sales Pty Limited,
120 Rothschild Avenue, Rosebery, NSW 2018, Australia.

Order No. CH68057
ISBN 1-84449-440-3
This book © Copyright 2004 by Chester Music.

Music engraved by Note-orious Productions Limited.
Compiled by Heather Ramage.

Printed in the United Kingdom.

Your Guarantee of Quality:
As publishers, we strive to produce every book to the highest commercial standards.
The music has been freshly engraved and carefully designed to minimise
awkward page turns to make playing from it a real pleasure.
Particular care has been given to specifying acid-free, neutral-sized
paper made from pulps which have not been elemental chlorine bleached.
This pulp is from farmed sustainable forests and was produced
with special regard for the environment.
Throughout, the printing and binding have been planned to ensure a sturdy,
attractive publication which should give years of enjoyment.
If your copy fails to meet our high standards, please inform us and we will gladly replace it.

www.musicsales.com

CHESTER MUSIC
part of the Music Sales Group

London/New York/Paris/Sydney/Copenhagen/Berlin/Madrid/Tokyo

Scott Joplin

Born in Texarkana, Texas in 1868, Scott Joplin was central to the creation of ragtime; a heady mix of syncopation and catchy melody. Initially seen as black music from the red-light areas and Vaudeville shows, it gradually gained respectability across America and reached Europe in 1900 when the band-leader Sousa, Joplin's white counterpart in American popular music, took arrangements of ragtime to Paris. Debussy and Stravinsky experimented with it in their piano music, and even Brahms intended to write a rag before he died.

Ragtime was a fusion of white marches and Western harmony with folk music and black rhythms from African drumming. In a piano rag the right hand plays off-beat melodies with a fluctuating sense of meter. This effect was difficult to master, and one early ragtime pianist called it "playing two different times at once". The influence of Sousa is found in the left hand, which imitates the 'oom-pah' bass-line of the march, providing a solid foundation for the syncopation above. The form of a rag mirrors the march, typically having four or five themes in two or more keys. Each theme is sixteen bars long and repeated. Although ragtime was written to dance to, it is known from early piano rolls and recordings that *rubato* and exaggerated speed changes were an accepted part of its performance.

Joplin was one of six children of an ex-slave father and a free mother. He was given free music lessons in his hometown then left home, aged fourteen, and became an itinerant musician moving from town to town to find work. After working in St Louis and Chicago he settled in Sedalia, Missouri in 1896. A quiet, thoughtful man, Joplin began to change attitudes among the 'respectable' classes towards ragtime. The 'sinful' syncopated music didn't seem so bad when played by this modest man. Gradually ragtime became popular with white people, which brought money and the chance for Joplin to publish his *Original Rags* in 1899. In that same year, publisher John Stark heard Joplin play at the Maple Leaf Club in Sedalia. Stark published the *Maple Leaf Rag* and with his financial backing it brought fame for Joplin, selling over a million copies across America.

In 1901 Stark, Joplin and his new wife Belle all moved back to St Louis. The *Peacherine Rag* and *The Easy Winners* were written in 1901, followed by *Elite Syncopations* and *The Entertainer* in 1902. Joplin tried to capture the sound of the tremolo style of the mandolin in *The Entertainer*. Also in 1902 he composed two marches, *Cleopha* and *A Breeze from Alabama*, still syncopated but retaining more of a march feel.

Relations between Joplin and Stark became strained as Joplin, against Stark's advice, wanted to try his hand at larger forms. He immersed himself in writing an opera, *The Guest of Honor*, which was only performed once in 1903. The score was then lost and its whereabouts remain unknown.

Three rags from 1904 show developments in Joplin's style. *The Cascades* depicts the water gardens at the World's Fair in St Louis with left hand octaves designed to sound like Sousa's trombones in its fourth theme. *The Sycamore* has a freer bass-line than usual and has some contrapuntal writing between the hands, while *The Chrysanthemum*, subtitled 'an African-American Intermezzo', is the first to have a contrasting, gentler mood in the trio section. In 1905 Joplin published his finest waltz *Bethena,* which has five elegant themes in five different keys. The syncopation of a melody in 3/4 time gives a subtle effect.

After an unsettled few years which included a split from his first wife and the death of his second, Freddie Alexander (to whom *The Chrysanthemum* is dedicated), Joplin settled again in New York in 1907. He met and married his third wife Lottie Stokes, and in 1908 he published *Pine Apple Rag* and *Fig Leaf Rag* as well as the instruction manual *The School of Ragtime*. *Solace* appeared in 1909, a Mexican tango-serenade full of romance and passion and in 1910 he wrote *Stop-Time Rag,* which incorporates the folk-dance practice of stopping the accompaniment and filling in the beat with foot stamps and slides. Despite the success of *Solace* and the *Paragon Rag*, whose banjo-style trio captured the sound of the plantations, ragtime was in trouble. Stark's business was in decline as other styles overshadowed ragtime. Joplin and Stark finally went their separate ways and Joplin submerged himself in opera, this time with the three-act *Treemonisha*.

Treemonisha dominated Joplin's last years. He began to suffer mood swings, and although he staged one performance of the opera in 1916, he had no costumes, props nor even a proper theatre. *Treemonisha* flopped, and Joplin was crushed. His wife finally had him committed to an asylum and he died a broken man on 1st April 1917. Joplin's music remained largely ignored until the 1970s ragtime revival, which included a successful production of *Treemonisha* on Broadway and the use of *The Entertainer* in the film *The Sting*. Shamefully neglected in his lifetime, Joplin now stands as a creative genius who left a unique legacy of a truly American popular style.

Kate Bradley.

Original Rags

Composed by Scott Joplin

Fine

Cleopha
(March & Two-Step)

Composed by Scott Joplin

Tempo di marcia (♩ = c.84)

Maple Leaf Rag

Composed by Scott Joplin

Tempo di marcia

Trio

Peacherine Rag

Composed by Scott Joplin

Not too fast

The Easy Winners
(A Ragtime Two-Step)

Composed by Scott Joplin

A Breeze From Alabama

(March & Two-Step)

Composed by Scott Joplin

Not fast

Elite Syncopations

Composed by Scott Joplin

Not fast

The Entertainer
(A Ragtime Two-Step)

Composed by Scott Joplin

(repeat R.H. 8va higher)

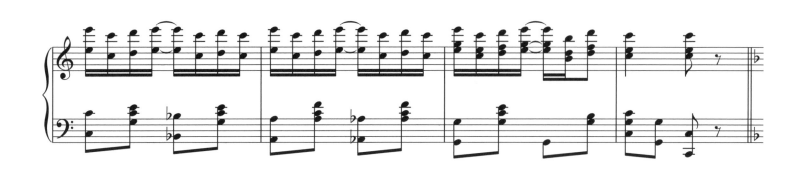

The Strenuous Life

(A Ragtime Two-Step)

Composed by Scott Joplin

Not fast

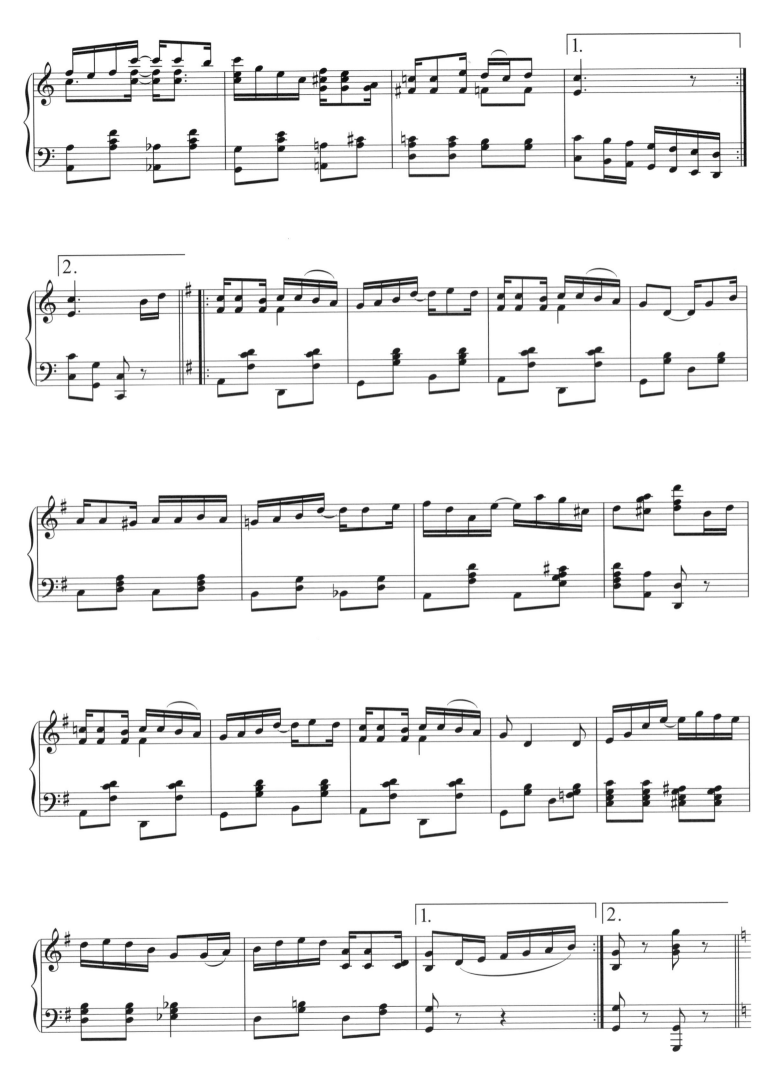

Weeping Willow
(A Ragtime Two-Step)

Composed by Scott Joplin

Not fast

The Sycamore

(A Concert Rag)

Composed by Scott Joplin

Tempo di marcia

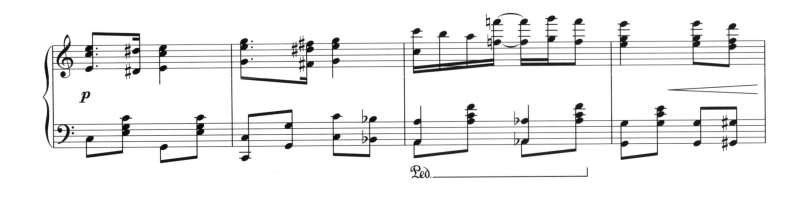

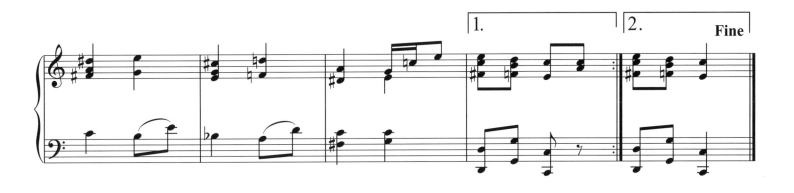

The Cascades

(A Rag)

Composed by Scott Joplin

Tempo di marcia

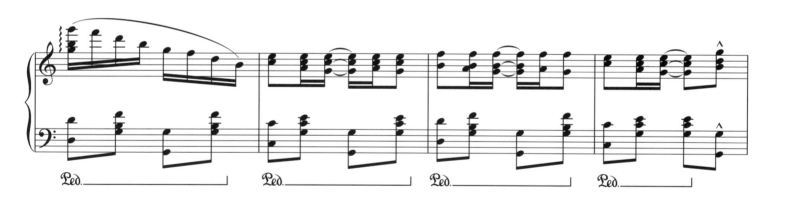

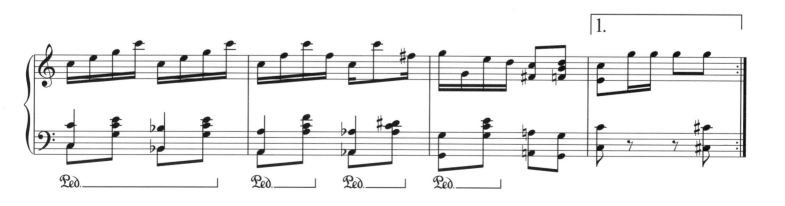

The Chrysanthemum
(An African-American Intermezzo)

Composed by Scott Joplin

Slow march tempo

Fig Leaf
(A High Class Rag)

Composed by Scott Joplin

Slow march tempo

Pine Apple Rag

Composed by Scott Joplin

Slow march tempo ♩ = 100

Paragon Rag

Composed by Scott Joplin

Slow march time

Trio

Stop-Time Rag

Composed by Scott Joplin

To get the desired effect of "Stop-Time," the pianist should *stamp* the heel of one foot heavily upon the floor on the word "stamp."
Do not raise the toe from the floor whilst stamping.

Fast or slow

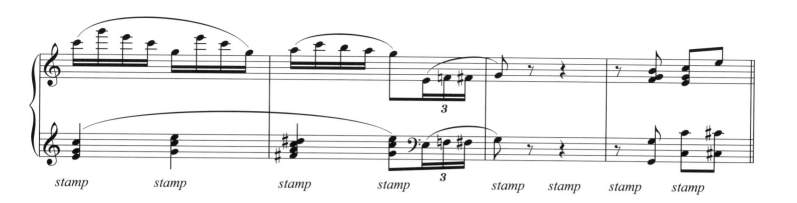

stamp *stamp* *stamp* *stamp* *stamp* *stamp* *stamp* *stamp*

stamp *stamp* *stamp* *stamp* *stamp* *stamp* *stamp* *stamp*

stamp *stamp* *stamp* *stamp* *stamp* *stamp* *stamp* *stamp*

stamp *stamp* *stamp* *stamp* *stamp* *stamp* *stamp* *stamp*

stamp *stamp* *stamp* *stamp* *stamp* *stamp* *stamp* *stamp* *stamp* *stamp*

stamp　*stamp*　　*stamp*　*stamp*　　*stamp*　*stamp*　　*stamp*　*stamp*　　*stamp*　*stamp*

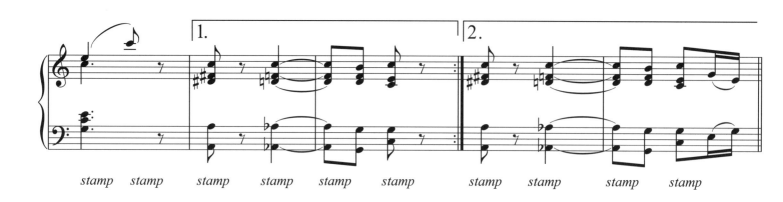

stamp　*stamp*　　*stamp*　*stamp*　*stamp*　*stamp*　　*stamp*　*stamp*　　*stamp*　*stamp*

stamp　　*stamp*　　*stamp*　　*stamp*　　*stamp*　*stamp*　　*stamp*　*stamp*

stamp　　*stamp*　　*stamp*　　*stamp*　　*stamp*　*stamp*　*stamp*　*stamp*

stamp　*stamp*　　*stamp*　*stamp*　　*stamp*　*stamp*　　*stamp*　*stamp*　　*stamp*　*stamp*

stamp *stamp* *stamp* *stamp* *stamp* *stamp* *stamp* *stamp*

stamp *stamp* *stamp* *stamp* *stamp* *stamp* *stamp* *stamp*

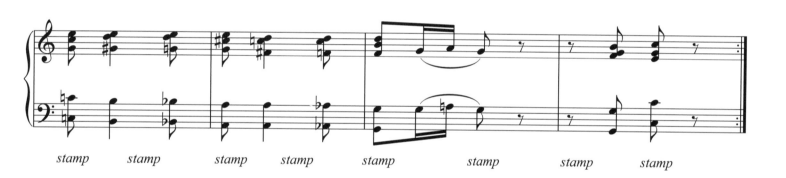

stamp *stamp* *stamp* *stamp* *stamp* *stamp* *stamp* *stamp*

stamp *stamp* *stamp* *stamp* *stamp* *stamp* *stamp* *stamp*

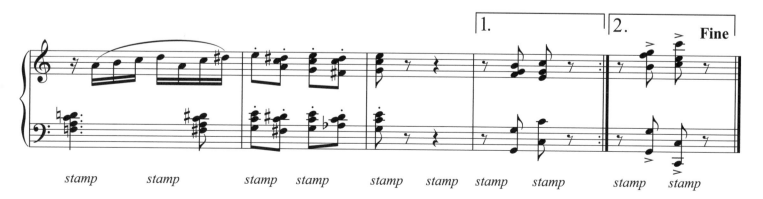

stamp *stamp* *stamp* *stamp* *stamp* *stamp* *stamp* *stamp* *stamp* *stamp*

Magnetic Rag

Composed by Scott Joplin

Tempo l'istesso

Bethena
(A Concert Waltz)

Composed by Scott Joplin

Tema
Valse tempo

rit. poco a poco

Valse cantabile
a tempo

cantabile

90

Solace

(A Mexican Serenade)

Composed by Scott Joplin

Very slow march time

a tempo

a tempo

a tempo

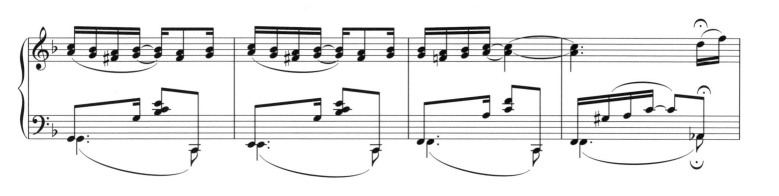

a tempo

4/05 (54822)

Also available
in *The Gold Series*

these beautifully presented albums
containing the most famous masterpieces
from the world's greatest composers.

BACH GOLD
Includes: Air On A G String,
Aria, Gavotte and Sleepers, Wake!
Order No. CH67067

BEETHOVEN GOLD
Includes: Symphony No.5,
Für Elise, Minuet in G and the
'Moonlight' Sonata.
Order No. CH65670

CHOPIN GOLD
Includes: All famous waltzes, nocturnes,
preludes and mazurkas as well as
excerpts from Piano Concerto No.1
and Sonata No.2 in B♭ Minor.
Order No. CH65681

HANDEL GOLD
Includes: Air (from Water Music),
The Arrival Of The Queen Of Sheba, and
Zadok The Priest (Coronation Anthem)
Order No. CH66792

MOZART GOLD
Includes: A Musical Joke,
Piano Concerto No.21 'Elvira Madigan',
Serenade in B♭ 'Gran Partita' and
Symphony No.40 in G minor.
Order No. CH65505

SCHUMANN GOLD
Includes: music from Album For The
Young, Forest Scenes and Night Pieces.
Order No. CH66863

TCHAIKOVSKY GOLD
Includes: 1812 Overture,
plus music from The Nutcracker,
Sleeping Beauty and
Swan Lake.
Order No. CH65692

*For more information on these and the thousands of
other titles available from Wise Publications and Chester Music, please contact:*

Music Sales Limited
Newmarket Road, Bury St Edmunds, Suffolk, IP33 3YB.
Tel: 01284 702600. Fax: 01284 768301.
www.musicsales.com